I0817286

Border Collies

by Julie Murray

Abdo Kids Jumbo is an Imprint of Abdo Kids
abdobooks.com

abdobooks.com

Published by Abdo Kids, a division of ABDO, P.O. Box 398166, Minneapolis, Minnesota 55439.

Printed in the United States of America, North Mankato, Minnesota.

102025

012026

Photo Credits: AdobeStock, Getty Images, Scinece Source, Shutterstock, Thinkstock

Production Contributors: Teddy Borth, Jennie Forsberg, Grace Hansen
Design Contributors: Candice Keimig, Julia Line

Library of Congress Control Number: 2025936493

Publisher's Cataloging-in-Publication Data

Names: Murray, Julie, author.

Title: Border collies / by Julie Murray

Description: Minneapolis, Minnesota : Abdo Kids, 2026 | Series: Dogs | Includes online resources and index.

Identifiers: ISBN 9798384907497 (lib. bdg.) | ISBN 9798384908197 (ebook) | ISBN 9798384908548 (read-to-me ebook)

Subjects: LCSH: Border collie--Juvenile literature. | Herding dogs--Juvenile literature. | Working dogs—Juvenile literature. | Dogs--Juvenile literature. | Dogs--Behavior--Juvenile literature. | Animal behavior--Juvenile literature.

Classification: DDC 636.7--dc23

Table of Contents

Border Collies

Border collies are bright and energetic **herding** dogs. They are always excited to have a job to do.

Border collies were first **bred** in the 1700s to **herd** sheep. This took place in a **border region** between Scotland and England. That is how they got "Border" in their name.

Scotland
England
Europe

Border collies are medium-sized dogs. They can weigh up to 50 pounds (22.7 kg) and stand 22 inches (56 cm) tall. Males are larger than females.

Border collies have a thick double coat. It is waterproof. Their coat can be rough or smooth. Their ears can flop forward or stand up straight.

Most Border collies are black with white markings. Others can be brown, blue, gold, and other colors with white markings. Some dogs can have a solid, tricolor, or merle-pattern coat.

Brown and white

Black and white

Gold and white

Tricolor

Grooming

Border collies need weekly brushing and an occasional bath. Their ears need to be cleaned and their nails should be trimmed regularly.

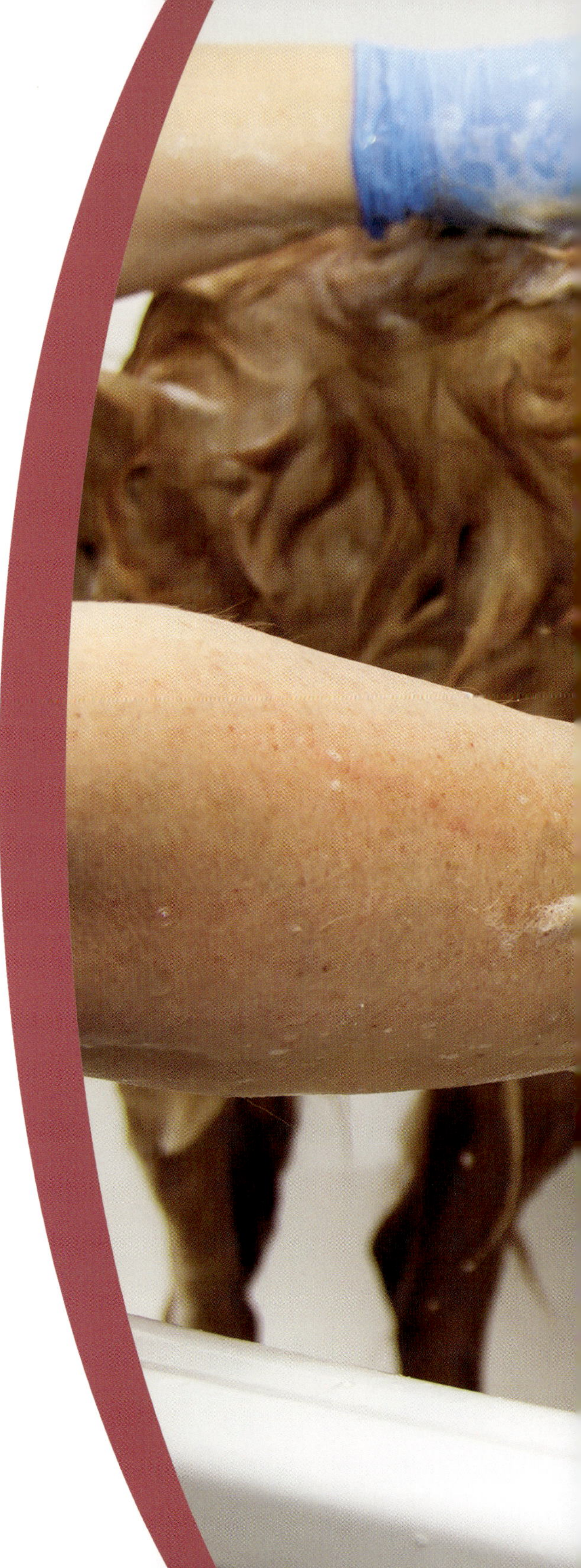

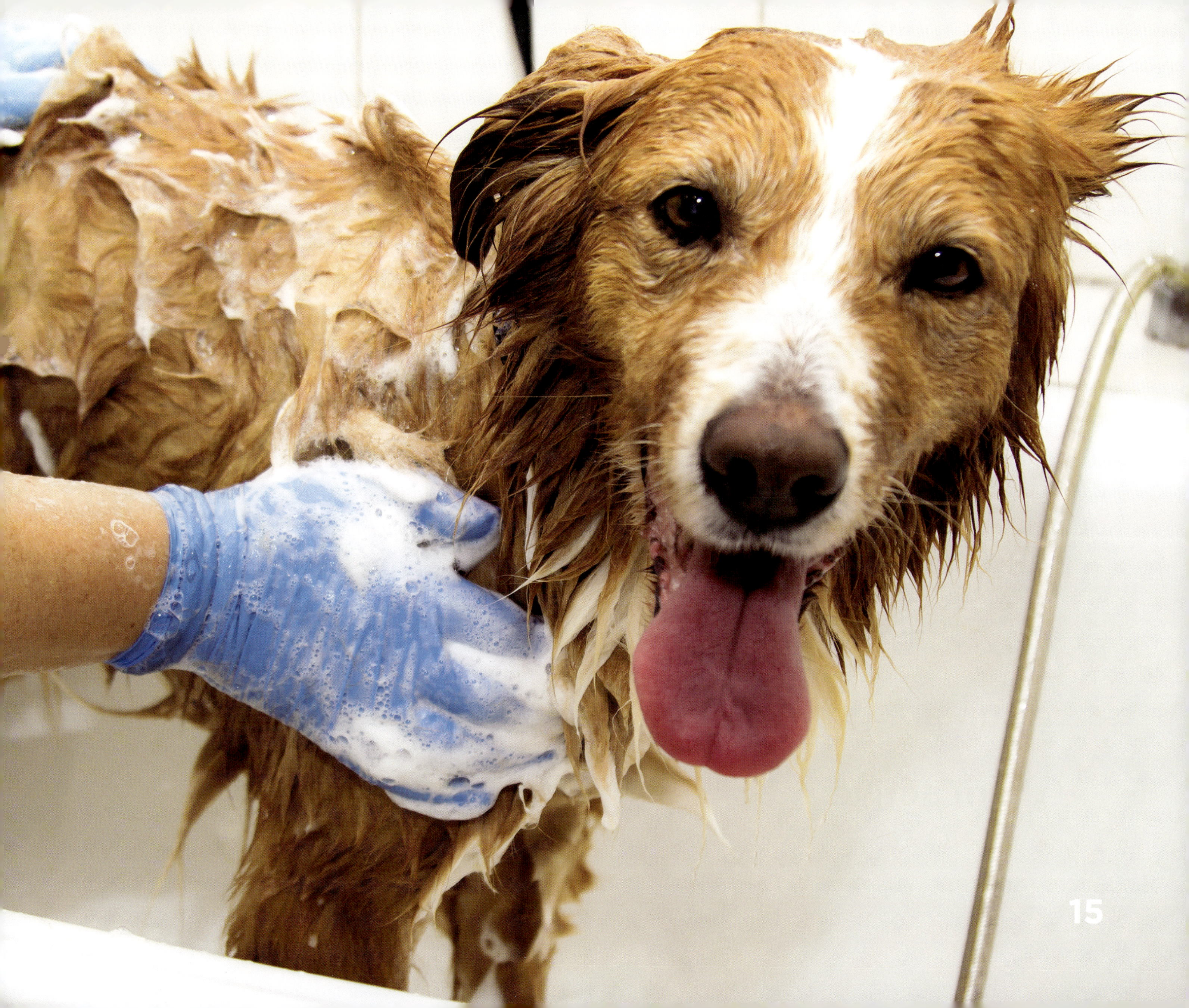

Exercise

Border collies have a lot of energy! They need physical and mental activities every day. Playing fetch or going for a run are great ways to keep them active.

Border collies enjoy having a job to do. They do well with **agility** training and are often at the top of the class!

Personality

Border collies are loving, **loyal**, and friendly. They make great family pets. They get along well with other animals and children.

More Facts

- Border collies stare down groups of animals to help control their movements.
- Border collies can make good **therapy dogs**. They can also be search and rescue dogs.
- The American Kennel Club officially recognized the **breed** in 1995. Border collies are members of the **Herding** Group.

Glossary

agility – a sport where handlers guide their dogs through a timed obstacle course.

border region – a large area of land that is near the boundary between two countries or regions.

bred – developed over time for a certain purpose.

breed – a particular kind of dog.

herd – to keep or move animals together.

loyal – giving or showing constant support to someone or something.

therapy dog – a well-trained dog that provides emotional support and comfort to people in different places, such as hospitals and schools.

Index

Visit **abdokids.com** to access crafts, games, videos, and more!

Use Abdo Kids code

DBK7497

or scan this QR code!